Earth, Earth, Earth, Hear The Word Of The Lord

(Jeremiah 22: 29)

And Who Is My Neighbor?

(Luke 10: 25-37)

By
Franklin B. Lovell Jr.

Table of Contents

Preface

At one time I was in a discussion with my uncle about Christianity and the bible. He started telling me about a couple of books that he had read, that had shown him a few discrepancies in the bible.

When I arrived home, I went to the library and borrowed one of those books and read through it. As I read through, I became upset with what I was reading. It was like everything that I had learned and read all my life about the bible wasn't quite correct.

I am not going to reference any passages that I came across because I don't want to create any sort of argument here. I just want to let the reader know of the path that led me to come up with this book.

I was sitting in my den, holding my bible in my hand when my frustration got the better of me. I looked over at my empty trash can and tossed my bible across the room into the trash can. I got up and walked out of the door.

Up to this point in my life I had already read the bible from cover to cover twice. The first time I read through it, I read it just as anyone would read any paperback novel. Reading it that way turned it into a page turner. I couldn't put it down. Well, almost. I still had work to do and chores, but I found myself reading at every opportunity.

Just like most paperback books, the Bible has history and heroes. It has drama, ambition and cutthroat activity along with backstabbing. People in authority taking advantage of their position and power. Sex and murder. War and slavery. It has greed and jealously. It flowed from book to book. Verse to verse. I would highly recommend everyone to read the bible in this manner. It is an awesome read.

The second time I read the bible I read through it very slowly. Sometimes I would just stop and ponder. I would get some other books such as biblical history to reference some of what I was reading. I read some chapters over. I confess that I did skip a lot of the begets. This reading took me well over a year. I found passages that I hadn't really noticed on my first read. Just like when you see a movie the second time, you notice parts that you don't remember when you first saw it.

I love the study of history. If I had life to live over again, I would want to be a history teacher. I don't care much about dates, such as remembering, "1492, Christopher Columbus sailed over the ocean blue. Dates are not all that important to me. It is the story. The story is fascinating and exciting. And just like in the bible, history has all the elements of your basic thriller movie or book. But in the case of the study of history, this thriller is of our ancestors.

Along with the study of history, I set out on the study of religion and mainly of Christianity. When you first start to study early Christian history, it starts off with a study of the Catholic Church. The early Popes and Emperor Charlemagne. The council of Nicaea. Consolidating of power and authority of the Church throughout Europe. From there you get to the first protestant, Martin Luther in Germany. There was a war fought between the Catholic church and Martin Luther's followers. You study the Crusades and the ugliness that came from that. There is the rebellion of King Henry the 8th of England against the Catholic church, and then more Protestant religions popping up. There is the, not just anger, but hatred that one belief has toward the other. They went around acting as though, "I am right in the way I believe and since you don't believe the way I do, you are evil."

When in my early twenties, my eyes were starting to open to more of the world. I had always heard of Lutherans and Methodists and Presbyterians and Baptist. Catholics, Mormons, Quakers and Calvinists. Jews and Buddhists' and Muslims.

My best friend in grammar school, in Chicago was Jewish. I had a friend there that was from Germany that was

Lutheran. We all were living in the middle of a large Catholic neighborhood. My family was from West Virginia. We were Baptist. My Boy Scout troop was sponsored and met at a Salvation Army church. To me all the religions were nothing more than like different clubs. No big deal. We were a bunch of kids that didn't care. We just wanted to play together and go to each other's birthday party.

And then in my early twenties while in the Marine Corps I started to notice the deep divisions that each of the Christian religions had toward one another and the divisions that the other world religions had toward one another. Each thinking they are the correct way and the others are completely wrong and are going to hell.

So, I thought to myself that they all can't be wrong, or all be completely right. That was when I set out to try to find some answers. That was when I started to do a study of religion, as I mentioned above.

So, now back to my having thrown my bible into my trash can. Having thrown my bible into the trash can really bothered me. It was on my mind constantly. A few weeks went by when a light dawned on me. The bible has a message throughout it. I saw that when I read through it. It doesn't matter if there are a few discrepancies in it. It is the story. The message. That message is what is important. So, I went over to my trash can and took my bible out.

I started on page one, with a pencil and paper and a typewriter. I started to read and pull out passages and verses that I was drawn to. I would type them up. This was my third time through the entire bible. I had pages and pages of typewritten material. There was no rhyme or reason to the order it was all in, just a bunch of typewritten bible verses.

I then took all of the typed written verses and passages and read them over several times. I could see the story. The message. It was there. I just had to put it in order. This job took me about a year. I sat in a little corner of a hallway in my house, when I wasn't working, and reordered all that I had originally typed out.

What I found was a message of love and kindness and generosity.

The following is not to replace the bible. It is the message that I see that the Christian bible and for that matter every religion on earth is telling its people.

The title that I picked is out of the King James Version, the book of Jeremiah, chapter 22, verse 29.

Earth, Earth, Earth, hear the word of the Lord.

The rest of it comes from the bible that I threw into the trash can. My favorite version. "The New English Bible".

The story in this book does not care what or which religion you may believe in.

The story in this book does not care if you are a true believer or an atheist.

This story is for anyone and for everyone.

All you have to do is hear, really hear what the story is saying.

There is an old saying that goes something like, "There are none so blind as those who refuse to see, there are none so deaf as those who refuse to hear." I truly hope that all that read this story have eyes to see with and ears to hear with.

Chapter 1

Earth, Earth, Earth hear the word of the Lord.[1] Look to me and be saved, you peoples from all corners of the earth; for I am God, there is no other.[2]

Come to me and listen to my words, hear me, and you shall have life.[3] It is the man who does right who is righteous…[4]

Turn, turn from your offenses, or your iniquity will be your downfall. Throw off the load of your past misdeeds; get yourselves a new heart and a new spirit.[5]

It may be that a wicked man gives up his sinful ways and keeps all my laws, doing what is just and right. That man shall live; he shall not die. None of the offense he has committed shall be remembered against him; he shall live because of his righteous deeds. Have I any desire, says the Lord God, for the death of a wicked man? Would I rather that he should mend his ways and live?[6]

Consider the man who is righteous and does what is just and right. He never lifts his eyes to idols, never dishonor's

---

[1] Jeremiah 22: 29 (King James Version)
[2] Isaiah 45: 22-23
[3] Isaiah 55: 3
[4] 1John 3: 7-8
[5] Ezekiel 18:30-32
[6] Ezekiel 18: 21-23

another man's wife. He oppresses no man, he returns the debtors pledge, he never robs. He gives bread to the hungry and clothes to those who have none. He never lends either at discount or at interest. He shuns injustice and deals fairly between man and man. He conforms to my statutes and loyally observes my laws. Such a man is righteous; he shall live. Says the Lord God.

He may have a son who is a man of violence and a cut-throat who turns his back on these rules. He obeys none of them, he dishonors another man's wife, he oppresses the unfortunate and the poor, he is a robber. He does not return the debtor's pledge, he lifts his eyes to idols and joins in abominable rites; he lends both at discount and at interest. Because he has committed all of these abominations he shall die, and his blood will be on his own head.

This man in turn may have a son who sees all of his father's sins; he sees, but he commits none of them. He never lifts his eyes to idols, never dishonors another man's wife. He oppresses no man, takes no pledge, does not rob. He gives bread to the hungry and clothes to those who have none. He shuns injustice, he never lends either at discount or at interest. He keeps my laws and conforms to my statutes. Such a man shall not die for his father's wrongdoing; he shall live.

His father may have been guilty of oppression and robbery and may have lived an evil life among his kinsfolk, and so has died because of his iniquity. You may ask, "Why is the son not punished for his father's iniquity?" Because he has always done what is just and right and has been careful to obey all my laws, therefore he shall live. It is the soul that sins, and no other, that shall die; a son shall not share a father's guilt, not a father his son's. The righteous man shall reap the fruit of his own righteousness, and the wicked man the fruit of his own wickedness.[7]

It may be that a righteous man turns back from his righteous ways and commits every kind of abomination that the wicked practice; shall he do this and live? No, none of his former righteousness will be remembered in his favor; he has broken his faith, he has sinned, and he shall die. If a righteous man turns from his righteousness, takes to evil ways and dies, it is because of these evil ways that he dies. Again, if a wicked man turns from his wicked ways and does what is just and right, he shall save his life. If he sees his offences as they are and turns his back on them all, then he shall live; he shall not die.[8]

This then is my word to you... Give up living like pagans with their good-for-nothing notions. Their wits are

---

[7] Ezekiel 18: 5-20
[8] Ezekiel 18: 24-28

3

beclouded, they are strangers to the life that is in God, because ignorance prevails among them, and their minds have grown hard as stone. Dead to all feeling, they have abandoned themselves to vice, and stop at nothing to satisfy their foul desires.[9]

...you must lay aside that old human nature which, deluded by its lusts, is sinking towards death. You must be made new in mind and spirit, and put on a new nature of Gods creating, which shows itself in the just and devout life called for by the truth... throw off false hood; speak the truth to each other... If you are angry, do not let anger lead you into sin; do not let sunset find you still nursing it...

The thief must give up stealing, and instead work hard and honestly with his own hands, so that he may have something to share with the needy.

No bad language must pass your lips, but only what is good and helpful to the occasion, so that it brings a blessing to those who hear it.

Be generous to one another, tender-hearted, forgiving one another...[10]

---

[9] Ephesians 4: 17-19
[10] Ephesians 4: 17-32

EACH OF US WILL HAVE TO ANSWER FOR HIMSELF

(Romans 14:12)

Chapter 2

This is the story of the birth of the Messiah. Mary his mother was betrothed to Joseph; before their marriage, she found that she was with child by the Holy Spirit. Being a man of principle… Joseph desired to have the marriage contract set aside quietly. He has resolved on this when an angel of the Lord appeared to him in a dream. "Joseph son of David;" said the angel, "do not be afraid to take Mary home with you as your wife. It is by the Holy Spirit that she has conceived this child. She will bear a son; and you shall give him the name Jesus…" All this happened in order to fulfill what the Lord declared through the prophet: The Virgin will conceive and bear a son, and he shall be called Emmanuel:" a name which means "God is with us." Rising from sleep Joseph did as the angel had directed him; he took Mary to be his wife but had no intercourse with her until her son was born. And he named the child Jesus.[11]

---

[11] Matthew 1: 18-25

Here is my servant, whom I uphold, my chosen one in whom I delight, I have bestowed my spirit upon him, and he will make justice shin on the nations. He will not call out or lift his voice high or make himself heard in the open street. He will not break a bruised reed, or snuff out a smoldering wick; he will make justice shine on every race, never faltering, never breaking down, he will plant justice on earth, while coasts and islands wait for his teaching.[12]

---

[12] Isaiah 42 1-4

Chapter 3

He grew up before the Lord[13] son though he was, he learned obedience in the school of suffering, and, once perfected, became the source of eternal salvation for all who obey him[14]...

Jesus replied, Follow me[15]... I do not speak on my own authority, but the Father who sent me has himself commanded me what to say and how to speak.[16] ...the world must be shown that I love the Father, and do exactly as he commands.[17] I know that his commands are eternal life.[18] In very truth, anyone who gives heed to what I say and put his trust in him who sent me has hold of eternal life, and does not come up for judgement, but has already passed from death to life.[19]

Only be sure that you act on the message and do not merely listen; for that would be to mislead yourselves. A man who listens to the message but never acts upon it is like one who looks in a mirror at the face nature gave him. He glances at himself and goes away, and at once forgets what

---

[13] Isaiah 53: 2
[14] Hebrews 5:7-10
[15] Matthew 8: 22
[16] John 12: 49-50
[17] John 14: 31
[18] John 12: 50
[19] John 5: 24-25

he looked like. But the man who looks closely into the perfect law, the law that makes us free, and who lives in its company, does not forget what he hears, but acts upon it; and that is the man who by acting will find happiness.

A man may think he is religious, but has no control over his tongue, he is deceiving himself; that man's religion is futile. The kind of religion which is without stain or fault in the sight of God our Father is this: to go to the help of orphans and widows in their distress and keep oneself untarnished by the world.[20]

My brothers, what use is it for a man to say he has faith when he does nothing to show it? Can that faith save him? Suppose a brother or a sister is in rags with not enough food for the day, and one of you says, "Good luck to you, keep yourselves warm, and have plenty to eat," but does nothing to supply their bodily needs, what good is that? So with faith; if it does not lead to action, it is in itself a lifeless thing.

But someone may object: "Here is one who claims to have faith and another who points to his deeds." To which I reply; "Prove to me that this faith you speak of is real though not accompanied by deeds, and by my deeds I will prove to you my faith." You have faith enough to believe

---

[20] James 1: 22-27

that there is one God. Excellent! The devils have faith like that, and it makes them tremble. But can you not see, you quibbler, that faith divorced from deeds is barren?[21] You see then that a man is justified by deeds and not by faith in itself.[22] As the body is dead when there is no breath left in it, so faith divorced from deeds is lifeless as a corpse.[23]

My brothers, not many of you should become teachers, for you may be certain that we who teach shall ourselves be judged with greater strictness. All of us often go wrong; the man who never says a wrong thing is a perfect character, able to bridle his whole being. If we put bits into horses' mouths to make them obey our will, we can direct their whole body. Or think of ships: large they may be, yet even when driven by strong gales they can be directed by a tiny rudder on whatever course the helmsman chooses. So with the tongue. It is a small member, but it can make huge claims.

What an immense stack of timber can be set ablaze by the tiniest spark! And the tongue is in effect a fire. It represents among our members the world with all its wickedness; it pollutes our whole being; it keeps the wheel of our existence red-hot, and its flames are fed by hell.

---

[21] James 2: 14-21
[22] James 2: 24
[23] James 2: 26

Beasts and birds of every kind, creatures that crawl on the ground or swim in the sea, can be subdued and have been subdued by mankind; but no man can subdue the tongue. It is an intractable evil, charged with deadly venom. We use it to sing the praises of our Lord and Father, and we use it to invoke curses upon our fellow-men who are made in God's likeness. Out of the same mouth comes praises and curses. My brothers, this should not be so. Does a fountain gush with both fresh and brackish water from the same opening? Can a fig-tree, my brothers, yield olives, or a vine figs? No more does saltwater yield fresh.

Who among you is wise or clever? Let his right conduct give practical proof of it, with the modesty that comes of wisdom. But if you are harboring bitter jealousy and selfish ambition in your hearts, consider whether your claims are not false, and a defiance of the truth. This is not the wisdom that comes from above; it is earth bound, sensual, demonic. For with jealousy and ambition come disorder and evil of every kind. But the wisdom from above is in the first place pure; and then peace loving, considerate, and open to reason; it is straightforward and sincere, rich in mercy and in kindly deeds that are its fruit. True justice is the harvest reaped by peacemakers from seeds sown in a spirit of peace.

What causes conflicts and quarrels among you? Do they not spring from the aggressiveness of your bodily desires?

You want something which you cannot have, and so you are bent on murder; you are envious, and cannot attain your ambition, and so you quarrel and fight.[24]

Next a word to you who have great possessions. Weep and wail over the miserable fate descending on you. Your riches have rotted; your fine clothes are moth-eaten; your silver and gold have rusted away, and their very rust will be evidence against you and consume your flesh like fire. You have piled up wealth in an age that is near its close. The wages you never paid to the men who mowed your fields are loud against you, and the outcry of the reapers has reached the ears of the Lord of Hosts. You have lived on earth in wanton luxury, fattening yourselves like cattle— and the day for slaughter has come. You have condemned the innocent and murdered him…[25] So sin must no longer reign in your mortal body, exacting obedience to the body's desires. You must no longer put its several parts at sin's disposal, as implements for doing wrong.[26]

…as you once yielded your bodies to the service of impurity and lawlessness, making for moral anarchy, so now you must yield them to the service of righteousness…[27]

---

[24] James (3: 1-18) (4: 1-2)
[25] James 5: 1-5
[26] Romans 6: 12-13
[27] Romans 6: 19

...offer your very selves to him: a living sacrifice, dedicated and fit for his acceptance, the worship offered by mind and heart. Adapt yourselves no longer to the pattern of this present world, but let your minds be remade and your whole nature thus transformed. Then you will be able to discern the will of God, and to know what is good, acceptable, and perfect.[28]

Let the wicked abandon their ways and evil men their thoughts...[29]

...the light has come into the world, but men preferred darkness to light because their deeds were evil. Bad men all hate the light and avoid it, for fear their practices should be shown up. The honest man comes to the light so that it may be clearly seen that God is in what he does.[30] Live like men who are at home in the daylight, for where light is, there all goodness springs up, all justice and truth. Try to find out what would please the Lord; take no part in the barren deeds of darkness, but show them up for what they are.[31]

---

[28] Romans 12: 1-2
[29] Isaiah 55:7
[30] John 3: 19-21
[31] Ephesians 5: 9-11

DOES THE LORD DESIRE OFFERINGS AND SACRIFICES AS HE DESIRES OBEDIENCE? OBEDIENCE IS BETTER THAN SACRIFICE, AND TO LISTEN TO HIM THAN THE FAT OF RAMS.

(I Samuel 15:22-23)

I WAS THERE TO BE SOUGHT BY A PEOPLE WHO DID NOT ASK, TO BE FOUND BY MEN WHO DID NOT SEEK ME. I SAID, "HERE AM I, HERE AM I," TO A NATION THAT DID NOT INVOKE ME BY NAME. I SPREAD OUT MY HANDS ALL DAY APPEALING TO AN UNRULY PEOPLE WHO WENT THEIR EVIL WAY.

(Isaiah 65: 1-3)

Chapter 4

And now a man came up and asked him, "Master, what good must I do to gain eternal life?" "Good?" said Jesus. "Why do you ask me about that? One alone is good. But you if you wish to enter into life, keep the commandments." "Which commandments?" he asked. Jesus answered, "do not murder; do not commit adultery; do not steal; do not give false evidence; honor your father and mother; and love your neighbor as yourself." The young man answered, "I have kept all these. Where do I still fall short?" Jesus said to him, "If you wish to go the whole way, go, sell your possessions, and give to the poor, and then you will have riches in heaven; and come, follow me." When the young man heard this, he went away with a heavy heart; for he was a man of great wealth.

Jesus said to his disciples, "I tell you this: a rich man will find it hard to enter the kingdom of Heaven.[32]

I tell you, unless a man has been born over again, he cannot see the Kingdom of God.[33] You must be made new in mind and spirit, and put on the new nature of God's

---

[32] Matthew 19: 16-23
[33] John 3: 3

creating, which shows itself in the just and devout life called for by the truth.[34]

As obedient children do not let your characters be shaped any longer by the desires you cherished in your days of ignorance. The one who called you is holy; like him, be holy in all your behavior, because Scripture says, "You shall be holy, for I am holy.[35]

In a word, as God's dear children, try to be like him[36] ...he called us to a dedicated life...[37]

Do not store up for yourselves treasure on earth, where it grows rusty and moth-eaten, and thieves break in to steal it. Store up treasure in heaven, where there is no moth and no rust to spoil it, no thieves to break in and steal. For where your heart is, there will your heart be also.[38]

For, as I have often told you, and now tell you with tears in my eyes, there are many whose way of life makes them enemies... They are heading for destruction, appetite is their god, and they glory in their shame. Their minds are set on earthly things.[39]

---

[34] Ephesians 4: 23-24
[35] I Peter 1: 13-16
[36] Ephesians 5: 1
[37] II Timothy 1:8
[38] Matthew 6: 19-21
[39] Philippians 3: 18-19

They think religion should yield dividends; and of course religion does yield high dividends, but only to the man whose resources are within him. We brought nothing into the world; for that matter we cannot take anything with us when we leave, but if we have food and covering we may rest content. Those who want to be rich fall into temptations and snares and many foolish harmful desires which plunges men into ruin and perdition. The love of money is the root of all evil things, and there are some who in reaching for it have wandered from the faith and spiked themselves on many thorny griefs. …you… must shun all this, and pursue justice, piety, fidelity, love, fortitude and gentleness.[40] Instruct those who are rich in those world's goods not to be proud and not to fix their hopes on so uncertain a thing as money… Tell them to do good and to grow rich in noble actions, to be ready to give away and to share and so acquire a treasure which will form a good foundation for the future. Thus they will grasp the life which is life indeed.[41]

Not everyone who calls me "Lord, Lord" will enter the kingdom of Heaven, but only those who do the will of my heavenly Father. When that day comes, many will say to me, "Lord, Lord, did we not prophesy in your name, cast out devils in your name, and in your name perform many

---

[40] I Timothy 6: 6-11
[41] I Timothy 6: 17-19

miracles?" Then I will tell them to their face, "I never knew you; out of my sight, you and your wicked ways!"[42] You say, "How rich I am! And how well I have done! I have everything I want." In fact, though you do not know it, you are the most pitiful wretch, poor, blind, and naked.[43]

Put no faith in princes, or in any man,…[44]Satan himself masquerades as an angel of light. It is therefore a simple thing for his agents to masquerade as agents of good.[45]

I know that when I am gone, savage wolves will come in among you and will not spare the flock. …there will be men coming forward who will distort the truth to induce the disciples to break away and follow them.[46]…some will desert from the faith and give their minds to subversive doctrines inspired by devils, through the specious falsehoods of men whose own conscience is branded with the devils sign.[47]

You must face the fact: the final age of this world is to be a time of troubles. Men will love nothing but money and self; they will be arrogant, boastful, and abusive; they will be implacable in their hatreds, scandal-mongers,

---

[42] Matthew 7: 21-23
[43] Revelation 3: 17-18
[44] Psalm 146: 3
[45] II Corinthians 11:15I
[46] Acts 20: 29-30
[47] I Timothy 4: 1

intemperate and fierce, strangers to all goodness, traitors, adventurers, swollen with self-importance.[48] ...They will not stand wholesome teaching, but will follow their own fancy and gather a crowd of teachers to tickle their ears. They will stop their ears to the truth.[49] They will be men... who preserve the outward form of religion, but are a standing denial of its reality. Keep clear of men like these.[50] They are of the world, and so therefore is their teaching; that is why the world listens to them. [51]

The kind of religion which is without stain or fault in the sight of God our Father is this: to... keep oneself untarnished by the world.[52] For the grace of God has dawned upon the world with healing for all mankind; and by it we are disciplined to renounce godless ways and worldly desires, and to live a life of temperance, honesty, and godliness...[53] ...with us therefore worldly standards have ceased to count.[54]

Make no mistake about this: if there is anyone among you who fancies himself wise—wise, I mean, by the standards of this passing age—he must become a fool to

---

[48] II Timothy 3: 1-4
[49] II Timothy 4: 3-4
[50] II Timothy 3: 4-5
[51] I John 4: 5
[52] James 1: 27
[53] Titus 2: 11-12
[54] II Corinthians 5: 16

gain true wisdom. For the wisdom of this world is folly in God's sight.[55]

If you take my words to heart and lay up my commands in your mind, giving your attention to wisdom and your mind to understanding, if you summon discernment to your aid and invoking understanding, if you seek her out like silver and dig for her like buried treasure, then you will understand …and attain the knowledge of God; for the Lord bestows wisdom and teaches knowledge and understanding.[56]

Then you will understand what is right and just and keep only to the good man's path; for wisdom will sink into your mind, and knowledge will be your heart's delight.[57]

Happy he who has found wisdom, and the man who has acquired understanding; for wisdom is more profitable than silver, and the gain she brings is better than gold. She is more precious than red coral, and all your jewels are no match for her. Long life is in her right hand, in her left hand are riches and honor. Her ways are pleasant and all her paths lead to prosperity. She is a staff of life to all who grasp her, and those who hold her fast and safe.[58]

---

[55] I Corinthians 3: 18-19
[56] Proverbs 2: 1-6
[57] Proverbs 2: 9-10
[58] Proverbs 3: 13-18

IT IS BETTER TO LISTEN TO A WISE MAN'S REBUKE THAN TO THE PRAISE OF FOOLS.

(Ecclesiastes 7:6)

Chapter 5

You have learned that our forefathers were told, Do not commit murder; anyone who commits murder must be brought to judgement." But what I tell you is this: Anyone who nurses anger against his brother must be brought to judgement. If he abuses his brother he must answer for it to the court; if he sneers at him he will have to answer for it in the fires of hell.[59]...if a man says, "I love God," while hating his brother, he is a liar. If he does not love his brother whom he has seen, it cannot be that he loves God whom he has not seen.[60]

You have learned that they were told, "Eye for an eye, tooth for a tooth." But what I tell you is this: Do not set yourself against the man who wrongs you.[61] For if you forgive others the wrongs they have done, your heavenly Father will also forgive you; but if you do not forgive others, then the wrongs you have done will not be forgiven by your Father.[62] The man who does not love is in the realm of death, for everyone who hates his brother is a murderer, and no murderer, has eternal life dwelling within him.[63]

---

[59] Matthew 5: 21-22
[60] I John 4: 20-21
[61] Matthew 5: 38-39
[62] Matthew 6: 14-15
[63] I John 3: 15

The Kingdom of Heaven, therefore, should be thought of in this way: There was once a king who decided to settle accounts with the men who served him. At the outset there appeared before him a man whose debt ran into millions. Since he had no means of paying, his master ordered him to be sold to meet the debt, with his wife, his children, and everything he had. The man fell prostrate at his master's feet. "Be patient with me," he said, "and I will pay in full;" and the master was so moved with pity that he let the man go and remitted the debt. But no sooner had the man gone out than he met a fellow servant who owed him a few pounds and catching hold of him he gripped him by the throat and said, "Pay me what you owe." The man fell at his fellow-servant's feet, and begged him, "Be patient with me, and I will pay you;" but he refused and had him jailed until he should pay the debt. The other servants were deeply distressed when they saw what had happened, and they went to their master and told him the whole story. He accordingly sent for the man. "You scoundrel!" he said to him; "I remitted the whole of your debt when you appealed to me; were you not bound to show your fellow-servant the same pity as I showed you?" Ans so angry was the master that he condemned the man to torture until he should pay the debt in full. And that is how my heavenly Father will deal with you, unless you forgive your brother from your hearts.[64]

You have learned that they were told, "Love your neighbor, hate your enemy." But what I tell you is this: Love your enemies (Bless those who curse you, do good to those who hate you) and pray for your persecutors; only so can you be children of your heavenly Father, who makes his sun rise on good and bad alike, and sends the rain on the honest and dishonest. If you love only those who love you, what reward can you expect? And if you greet only your brothers, what is there extraordinary about that? Even the heathen do as much. There must be no limit to your goodness...[65] Never cease to love... Remember to show hospitality. There are some who, by so doing have entertained angels without knowing it.[66]

If your enemy is hungry, feed him; if he is thirsty, give him a drink; ...Do not let evil conquer you, but use good to defeat evil.[67]

I may have the gift of prophecy and know every hidden truth; I may have faith strong enough to move mountains; but if I have no love, I am nothing. I may dole out all I

---

[64] Matthew 18: 23-35
[65] Matthew 5: 43-48
[66] Hebrews 13: 1-2
[67] Romans 12: 20-21

possess, or even give my body to be burnt, but if I have no love, I am none the better.

Love is patient; love is kind and envies no one. Love is never boastful, nor conceited, not rude; never selfish, not quick to take offence. Love keeps no score of wrongs; does not gloat over other men's sins, but delights in the truth.[68]

Then one of the lawyers, who had been listening to these discussions and had noted how well he answered, came forward and asked him, "Which commandment is first of all?" Jesus answered, "The first is, "Hear O Israel: The Lord our God is the only Lord; love the Lord your God withal your heart, with all your soul, with all your mind, and with all your strength." The second is this: "Love your neighbor as yourself." There is no other commandment greater than these." The lawyer said to him, "Well said, Master. You are right in saying that God is one and beside him there is no other. And to love him with all your heart, all your understanding, and all your strength, and to love your neighbor as yourself—that is far more than any burnt offerings or sacrifices." When Jesus saw how sensibly he answered, he said to him, you are not far from the kingdom of God.[69]

---

[68] I Corinthians 12: 2-6
[69] Mark 12: 28-34

Do not suppose that I have come to abolish the Law and the prophets; I did not come to abolish, but to complete. I tell you this: so long as heaven and earth endure, not a letter, not a stroke, will disappear from the Law until that must happen has happened.[70]

He who loves his neighbor has satisfied every claim of the law. For the commandments, "Thou shalt not commit adultery, thou shalt not kill, thou shalt not steal, thou shalt not covet', and any other commandment there may be, are all summed up in the one rule, 'Love your neighbor as yourself.' Love cannot wrong a neighbor; therefore the whole law is summed up in love.[71]

'Always treat others as you would like them to treat you: That is the law and the prophets.[72]

Love will never come to an end. Are there prophets? Their work will be over. Are there tongues of ecstasy? They will cease. Is there knowledge? It will vanish away; for our knowledge and our prophecy alike are partial, and the partial vanishes when wholeness comes. When I was a child, my speech, my outlook, and my thoughts were all childish. When I grew up, I had finished with childish things. Now we see only puzzling reflections in a mirror,

---

[70] Matthew 5: 17-18
[71] Romans 13: 8-10
[72] Matthew 7: 12

but then we shall see face to face. My knowledge now is partial; then it will be whole, like Gods knowledge of me. In a word, there are three things that last forever: faith, hope and love; but the greatest is love.[73]

[73] Corinthians 13: 8-13

*WILL ALL BE WELL WHEN HE EXAMINES YOU! WILL YOU
QUIBBLE WITH HIM AS YOU QUIBBLE WITH A MAN?*

(Job 13:9)

*MAN, YOUR FELLOW-COUNTRYMEN GATHER IN GROUPS
AND TALK OF YOU UNDER WALLS AND IN DOORWAYS AND
SAY TO ONE ANOTHER, "LET US GO AND SEE WHAT MESSAGE
THERE IS FROM THE LORD." SO MY PEOPLE WILL COME
CROWDING IN, AS PEOPLE DO, AND SIT DOWN IN FRONT OF
YOU. THEY WILL HEAR WHAT YOU HAVE TO SAY, BUT THEY
WILL NOT DO IT. "FINE WORDS!" THEY WILL SAY, BUT THEIR
HEARTS ARE SET ON SELFISH GAIN. YOU ARE NO MORE TO
THEM THAN A SINGER OF FINE SONGS WITH A LOVELY
VOICE, OR A CLEVER HARPIST: THEY WILL LISTEN TO WHAT
YOU SAY BUT WILL CERTAINLY NOT DO IT.*

(Ezekiel 33:30-33)

*WHY DO THE WICKED PROSPER AND TRAITORS LIVE AT
EASE? THOU HAST PLANTED THEM AND THEIR ROOTS
STRIKE DEEP, THEY GROW UP AND BEAR FRUIT, THOU ART
EVER ON THEIR LIPS, YET FAR FROM THEIR HEARTS.*

(Jeremiah 12:2)

Chapter 6

When you are having a party for lunch or supper, do not invite your friends, your brothers or other relations, or your rich neighbors; they will only ask you back again and so you will be repaid. But when you give a party, ask the poor, the crippled, the lame, and the blind; and so find happiness. For they have no means of repaying you; but you will be repaid on the day when good me rise from the dead.[74]

A lawyer came forward to put this question to him: "Master, what must I do to inherit eternal life?" Jesus said, "What is written in the Law? What is your reading of it? He replied. "Love the Lord your God with all your heart, with all your soul, with all your strength, and with all your mind; and your neighbor as yourself." That is the right answer," said Jesus; "do that and you will live."

But he wanted to vindicate himself, so he said to Jesus, "And who is my neighbor?" Jesus replied, "A man was on his way from Jerusalem down to Jericho when he fell in with robbers, who stripped him, beat him, and went off leaving him half dead. It so happened that a priest was going down by the same road; but when he saw him, he went past on the other side. So too a Levite came to the place, and when he saw him went past on the other side. But a

---

[74] Luke 14: 12-14

Samaritan who was making the journey came upon him, and when he saw, him was moved to pity. He went up and bandaged his wounds, bathing them with oil and wine. Then he lifted him onto his own beast, brought him to an inn, and looked after him there. Next day he produced two silver pieces and gave them to the innkeeper, and said, "Look after him; and if you spend anymore, I will repay on my way back." Which of these three do you think was neighbor to the man who fell into the hands of the robbers?" He answered, "The one who showed him kindness." Jesus said, "Go and do as he did."[75]

When the Son of Man comes in his glory and all the angels with him, he will sit in state on his throne, with all the nations gathered before him. He will separate men into two groups, as a shepherd separates the sheep from the goats, and he will place the sheep on his right hand and the goats on his left. Then the king will say to those on his right hand, "You have my Fathers blessing; come enter and possess the kingdom that has been ready for you since the world was made. For when I was hungry, you gave me food; when thirsty, you gave me drink; when I was a stranger you took me into your home, when naked you clothed me; when I was ill you came to my help, when in prison you visited me." Then the righteous will reply, "Lord, when was it that

---

[75] Luke 10: 25-37

we saw you hungry and fed you, or thirsty and gave you drink, a stranger and took you home or naked and clothed you? When did we see you ill or in prison and come to visit you?" and the king will answer, "I tell you this: anything you did for one of my brothers here, however humble, you did for me." Then he will say to those on his left hand, "The curse is upon you; go from my sight to the eternal fire that is ready for the devil and his angels. For when I was hungry you gave me nothing to eat, when thirsty nothing to drink; when I was a stranger you gave me no home, when naked you did not clothe me; when I was ill and in prison you did not come to my help." And they too will reply, "Lord, when was it that we saw you hungry or thirsty or a stranger or naked or ill or in prison, and did nothing for you?" And he will answer, "I tell you this: anything you did not do for one of these, however humble, you did not do for me." And they will go away to eternal punishment, but the righteous will enter eternal life."[76]

You know that in the world the recognized rulers lord it over their subjects, and their great men make them feel the weight of authority. That is not the way with you; among you, whoever wants to be great must be your servant, and whoever wants to be first must be the willing slave of all.

---

[76] Matthew 25: 31-46

For even the Son of Man did not come to be served but to serve...[77]

Be careful not to make a show of your religion before men; if you do no reward awaits you in your Father's house in heaven.

Thus, when you do some act of charity, do not announce it with a flourish of trumpets, as the hypocrites do in synagogue and in the streets to win admiration from men. I tell you this: they have their reward already. No; when you do some act of charity, do not let your left hand know what your right hand is doing; your good deed must be secret, and your Father who sees what is done in secret will reward you.

Again, when you pray, do not be like the hypocrites; they love to say their prayers standing up in the synagogue and at the street-corners, for everyone to see them. I tell you this: they have their reward already. But when you pray, go into a room by yourself, shut the door, and pray to your Father who sees what is secret will reward you.

In your prayers do not go on babbling on like the heathen, who imagines that the more they say the more

---

[77] Mark 10: 42-45

likely they are to be heard. Do not imitate them. Your Father knows what your needs are before you ask him.[78]

And here is another parable that he told. It was aimed at those who were sure of their own goodness and looked down on everyone else.

"Two men went up to the temple to pray, one a Pharisee and the other a Tax-gatherer. The Pharisee stood up and prayed thus: "I thank thee O God, that I am not like the rest of man, greedy, dishonest, adulterous; or, for that matter, like this tax-gatherer. I fast twice a week; I pay tithes on all that I get." But the other kept his distance and would not even raise his eyes to heaven, but beat upon his breast, saying, "O God, have mercy on me, sinner that I am." It was this man, I tell you, and not the other, who went home acquitted of his sins. For everyone who exalts himself will be humbled; and whoever humbles himself will be exalted."[79]

'Alas, alas for you, lawyers and Pharisees, hypocrites that you are![80] You are like tombs covered with whitewash; they look well from outside, but inside they are full of dead men's bones and all kinds of filth. So it is with you: outside

---

[78] Matthew 6: 1-8
[79] Luke 18: 9-14
[80] Matthew 23: 13

you look like honest men, but inside you are brim-full of hypocrisy and crime.[81]

…you must not be called "rabbi"; for you have one Rabbi, and you are all brothers. Do not call any man on earth "father"; for you have one Father, and he is in heaven. Nor must you be called "teacher"; you have one Teacher, the Messiah. The greatest among you must be your servant. For whoever exalts himself will be humbled; and whoever humbles himself will be exalted.[82]

…my brothers, do not use oaths, whether 'by heaven' or 'by earth' or by anything else. When you say yes or no, let it be plain 'YES or NO'…[83]

When Jesus had finished… the people were astonished at his teaching; unlike their own teachers he taught with a note of authority[84]

I shall not talk much longer with you, for the Prince of this world approaches. He has no rights over me; but the world must be shown that I love the Father and do exactly as he commands.[85]

---

[81] Matthew 23: 27-28
[82] Matthew 23: 8-12
[83] James 5: 12
[84] Matthew 7: 28-29
[85] John 14: 30-31

Chapter 7

Jesus then came with his disciples to a place called Gethsemane. He said to them, "Sit here while I go over there to pray." He took with him Peter and the two sons of Zebedee. Anguish and dismay came over him, and he said to them, "My heart is ready to break with grief. Stop here and stay awake with me." He went on a little, fell on his face in prayer, and said, "My Father, if it is possible, let this cup pass me by. Yet not as I will but as thou wilt."

He came to the disciples and found them asleep; and he said to Peter. "What! Could none of you stay awake with me one hour? Stay awake and pray that you may be spared the test. The spirit is willing, but the flesh is weak."

He went away a second time, and prayed: "My Father, if it is not possible for this cup to pass me by without my drinking it, thy will be done." He came again and found them asleep, for their eyes were heavy. So he left them and went away again; and he prayed the third time, using the same words as before.

Then he came to the disciples and said to them, "Still sleeping? Still taking your ease? The hour has come! The Son of Man is betrayed to sinful men. Up, let us go forward; the traitor is upon us."

While he was still speaking, Judas…appeared; with him was a great crowd armed with swords and cudgels, sent by the chief priests and the elders of the nation. The traitor gave them this sign: 'The one I kiss is your man; seize him' and stepping forward at once, he said, 'Hail, Rabbi!', and kissed him. Jesus replied, 'Friend, do what you are here to do,' They then came forward, seized Jesus, and held him fast.[86]

…Jesus spoke to the crowd: Do you take me for a bandit, that you have come out with swords and cudgels to arrest me? Day after day I sat teaching in the temple, and you did not lay hands on me…

Jesus was led off under arrest to the house of Caiaphas the High Priest, where the lawyers and elders were assembled.[87]

The chief priests and the whole Council tried to find some evidence against Jesus to warrant a death-sentence but failed to find any. Many gave false evidence against him but their statements did not tally. Some stood up and gave false evidence against him to this effect: "We heard him say, "I will pull down this temple, made with human hands, and in three days I will build another, not made with hands." But even on this point their evidence did not agree.

---

[86] Matthew 26: 36-50
[87] Matthew 26 55-57

Then the High Priest stood up in his place and questioned Jesus: "Have you no answer to the charges that these witnesses bring against you?" But he kept silence; he made no reply.

Again, the High Priest questioned him: "Are you the Messiah, the Son of the Blessed One?" Jesus said, "I am and you will see the Son of Man seated at the right hand of God and coming with the clouds of heaven." Then the High Priest tore his robes and said, "Need we call further witnesses? You have heard blasphemy. What is your opinion?" Their judgement was unanimous: that he was guilty and should be put to death.[88]

Then they spat in his face and struck him with their fists; and others said, as they beat him, "Now, Messiah, if you are a prophet, tell us who hit you."[89]

When morning came, the chief priests and the elders of the nation met in conference to plan the death of Jesus. They then put him in chains and led him away, to hand him over to Pilate, the Roman Governor.[90]

Jesus was now before the Governor; and as he stood there...[91] They opened the case against him by saying, "We

---

[88] Mark 14: 55-65
[89] Matthew 26: 67-68
[90] Matthew 27: 1-2
[91] Matthew 27: 11

found this man subverting our nation, opposing the payment of taxes to Caesar, and claiming to be Messiah, a king."[92]

Are you the king of the Jews/", he asked. Jesus said, "Is that your own idea or have others suggested it to you?" "What am I a Jew?" said Pilate. "Your own nation and their chief priests have brought you here before me. What have you done?" Jesus replied, "My kingdom does not belong to this world. If it did, my followers would be fighting to save me from arrest by the Jews. My kingly authority comes from elsewhere." "You are a king, then?" said Pilate. Jesus answered, "King is your word. My task is to bear witness to the truth. For this was I born; for this I came into the world, and all who are not deaf to truth listen to my voice." Pilate said, "What is truth?", and with those words went out again to the Jews. "For my part," he said, "I find no case against him.[93]

But they insisted: "His teaching is causing disaffection among the people all through Judaea. It started from Galilee and has spread as far as this city.

When Pilate heard this, he asked if the man was a Galilean, and on learning that he belonged to Herod's jurisdiction he remitted the case to him, for Herod was also

---

[92] Luke 23: 1-2
[93] John 18: 33-39

in Jerusalem at that time. When Herod saw Jesus, he was greatly pleased; having heard about him, he had long been wanting to see him, and had been hoping to see some miracle performed by him. He questioned him at some length without getting any reply; but the chief priests and lawyers appeared and pressed the case against him vigorously. Then Herod and his troops treated him with contempt and ridicule and sent him back to Pilate dressed in a gorgeous robe.

Pilate now called together the chief priests, councilors, and people, and said to them, "You brought this man before me on a charge of subversion. But, as you see, I have myself examined him in your presence and found nothing in him to support your charges. No more did Herod, for he has referred him back to us. Clearly he has done nothing to deserve death. I therefore propose to let him off with a flogging."[94]

Pilate now took Jesus and had him flogged; and the soldiers plaited a crown of thorns and placed it on his head, and robed him in a purple cloak. Then time after time they came up to him, crying, 'Hail, King of the Jews!', and struck him on the face.

---

[94] Luke 23: (5-11) (13-16)

Once more Pilate came out and said to the Jews, 'Here he is; I am bringing him out to let you know that I find no case against him; and Jesus came out, wearing the crown of thorns and the purple cloak. 'Behold the Man!' said Pilate. The chief priests and their henchmen saw him and shouted, 'Crucify! Crucify! 'Take him and crucify him yourselves,' said Pilate; 'for my part I find no case against him.' The Jews answered, 'We have a law; and by that law he ought to die, because he has claimed to be Son of God.'

When Pilate heard that, he was more afraid than ever, and going back into his headquarters he asked Jesus, 'Where do you come from?' But Jesus gave him no answer. 'Do you refuse to speak to me?' said Pilate. "Surely you know that I have authority to release you, and I have authority to crucify you?' You would have no authority at all over me', Jesus replied, 'if it had not been granted you from above; and therefore the deeper guilt lies with the man who handed me over to you.' From that moment Pilate tried hard to release him…[95]

At the festival season it was the Governor's custom to release one prisoner chosen by the people. There was then in custody a man of some notoriety, called Jesus Bar-Abbas. When they assembled Pilate said to them, 'Which would

---

[95] John 19: 1-12

you like me to release to you –Jesus Bar-Abbas, or Jesus called Messiah?'

While sitting in court a message came to him from his wife: 'Have nothing to do with that innocent man; I was much troubled on his account in my dreams last night.'

Meanwhile the chief priests and elders had persuaded the crowd to ask for the release of Bar-Abbas and to have Jesus put to death. So when the Governor asked, 'Which of the two do you wish me to release to you?' they said, 'Bar-Abbas.' 'Then what am I to do with Jesus called Messiah?' asked Pilate; and with one voice they answered, 'Crucify him!' 'Why, what harm has he done?' Pilate asked; but they shouted all the louder, 'Crucify him!'[96] If you let this man go, you are no friend to Caesar; any man who claims to be a king is defying Caesar." When Pilate heard what they were saying, he brought Jesus out and took his seat on the tribunal… Pilate said to the Jews, here is your king." They shouted, "Away with him! Away with him! Crucify him!" "Crucify your king?" said Pilate. "We have no king but Caesar", the Jews replied. Then at last, to satisfy them, he handed Jesus over to be crucified.[97]

---

[96] Matthew 27: 15-23
[97] John 19: 12-16

Chapter 8

They led him away to be crucified. On their way out they met a man from Cyrene, Simon by name, and pressed him into service to carry his cross. So they came to a place called Golgotha (which means 'Place of a skull') and there he was offered a draught of wine mixed with gall; but when he had tasted it he would not drink.

After fastening him to the cross they divided his clothes among them by casting lots, and then sat down to watch.[98]

Pilate wrote an inscription to be fastened to the cross; it read, 'Jesus of Nazareth King of the Jews.' This inscription was read by many Jews because the place where Jesus was crucified was not far from the city, and the inscription was in Hebrew, Latin, and Greek. Then the Jewish chief priest said to Pilate, 'You should not write "King of the Jews"; write, "He claimed to be king of the Jews." Pilate replied, 'What I have written, I have written.'[99]

The hour of the crucifixion was nine in the morning. Two bandits were crucified with him, one on his right and the other on his left.[100]

---

[98] Matthew 27: 32-36
[99] John 19: 19-22
[100] Mark 15: 26-27

The people stood looking on, and their rulers jeered at him: He saved others: now let him save himself, if this is God's Messiah, his chosen.' The soldiers joined in the mockery and came forward offering him sour wine. 'If you are the king of the Jews,' they said, 'save yourself.'

One of the criminals who hung there with him taunted him: 'Are not you the Messiah? Save yourself, and us.' But the other rebuked him: 'Have you no fear of God? You are under the same sentence as he. For us it is plain justice; we are paying the price for our misdeeds; but this man has done nothing wrong.' And he said, 'Jesus, remember me when you come to your throne.'[101] …meanwhile near the cross where Jesus hung stood his mother, with her sister, Mary wife of Clopas, and Mary of Magdala. Jesus saw his mother, with the disciple whom he loved standing beside her. He said to her, Mother, there is your son'; and to the disciple, 'There is your mother'; and from that moment the disciple took her into his home.[102]

At midday a darkness fell over the whole land, which lasted till three in the afternoon; and at three Jesus cried aloud, "Eli, Eli, lema sabachthani?', which means, 'My God, my God, why hast thou forsaken me?' Some of the bystanders, on hearing this, said, 'Hark, he is calling Elijah.'

---

[101] Luke 23: 35-43
[102] John 19: 25-27

A man ran and soaked a sponge in sour wine and held it to his lips on the end of a cane. 'Let us see' he said, 'if Elijah will come to take him down.'[103]

My God, my God, why hast thou forsaken me and art so far from saving me, from heeding my groans? O my God, I cry in the day-time but thou dost not answer, in the night I cry but get no respite. And yet thou art enthroned in holiness, thou art he whose praises Israel sings. In thee our fathers put their trust; they trusted, and thou didst rescue them. Unto thee they cried and were delivered; in thee they trusted and were not put to shame.

But I am a worm, not a man, abused by all men, scorned by the people. All who see me jeer at me, make mouths at me and wag their heads: "He threw himself on the Lord for rescue; let the Lord delver him, for he holds him dear!!"

But thou art he who drew me from the womb, who laid me at my mother's breast. Upon thee was I cast at birth; from my mother's womb thou hast been my God.

Be not far from me, for trouble is near, and I have

[103] Mark 15: 33-37

no helper. A herd of bulls surrounds me great bulls of Bashan beset me. Ravening and roaring lions open their mouths wide against me.

My strength drains away like water and all my bones are loose. My heart has turned to wax and melts within me. My mouth is dry as a potsherd, and my tongue sticks to my jaw.

I am laid low in the dust of death. The huntsmen are all about me; a band of ruffians rings me round, and they have hacked off my hands and feet.

I tell my tale of misery, while they look and gloat. They share out my garments among them and cast lots for my clothes. But do not remain so far away, O Lord; O my help, hasten to my aid. Deliver my very self from the sword, my precious life from the axe. Save me from the lion's mouth, my poor body from the horns of the wild ox.

I will declare thy fame to my brethren; I will praise thee in the midst of the assembly. Praise him, you who fear the Lord; all you sons of Jacob, do him honor; stand in awe of him, all sons of Israel. For he has not scorned the downtrodden, nor shrunk in loathing from his plight, nor hidden his face from him, but gave heed to him when he cried out.

Thou dost inspire my praise in the full assembly; and I will pay my vows before all who fear thee. Let the humble eat and be satisfied. Let all the ends of the earth remember and turn again to the Lord; let all families of the nation's bow down before him.

For kingly power belongs to the Lord, and dominion over the nations is his.

How can those buried in the earth do him homage; how can those who go down to the grave vow before him?

But I shall live for his sake, my posterity shall serve him. This shall be told of the Lord to future generations; and they shall justify him, declaring to a people yet unborn that this was his doing.[104]

---

[104] Psalms 22: 1-31

...Jesus, aware that all had now come to this appointed end... he said, 'It is accomplished!'[105] Then Jesus gave out a loud cry and said "Father, into thy hands I commit my spirit'; and with these words he died.[106]

At that moment the curtain of the temple was torn from top to bottom. There was an earthquake, the rocks split...And when the centurion and his men who were keeping watch over Jesus saw the earthquake and all that was happening, they were filled with awe, and they said, 'Truly this man was a son of God.'[107]

When the evening fell, there came a man of Arimathea, Joseph by name, who was a man of means, and had himself become a disciple of Jesus. He approached Pilate and asked for the body of Jesus; and Pilate gave orders that he should have it. Joseph took the body, wrapped it in a clean linen sheet, and laid it in his own unused tomb, which he had cut out of the tock; he then rolled a large stone against the entrance, and went away. Mary of Magdala was there, and the other Mary, sitting opposite the grave.[108]

Next day, the chief priests and the Pharisees came in a body to Pilate. "Your Excellency," they said, "we recall

---

[105] John 19: 28-30
[106] Luke 23: 46
[107] Matthew 27: 50-54
[108] Matthew 27: 57-61

how that imposter said while he was still alive, "I am to be raised after three days." So, will you give orders for the grave to be made secure until the third day? Otherwise, his disciples may come, steal the body, and then tell the people that he has been raised from the dead; and the final deception will be worse than the first." "You may have your guard," said Pilate; "go and make secure as best you can." So, they went and made the grave secure; they sealed the stone and left the guard in charge.

The sabbath was over, and it was about daybreak on Sunday, when Mary of Magdala and the other Mary came to look at the grave. Suddenly there was a violent earthquake; and an angel of the Lord descended from heaven; he came to the stone and rolled it away and sat himself down on it. His face shown like lightning; his garments were white as snow. At the sight of him the guards shook with fear and lay like the dead.

The angel then addressed the woman: "You," he said, "have nothing to fear. I know you are looking for Jesus who was crucified. He is not here; he has been raised again, as he said he would be. Come and see the place where he was laid, and then go quickly and tell his disciples: "He has been raised from the dead and is going on before you into Galilee; there you will see him." That is what I had to tell you."

They hurried away from the tomb in awe and great joy and ran to tell the disciples. Suddenly Jesus was there in their path. He gave them his greeting, and they came up and clasped his feet, falling prostrate before him. Then Jesus said to them, "Do not be afraid. Go and take word to my brothers that they are to leave for Galilee. They will see me there."

The woman had started on their way when some of the guard went into the city and reported to the chief priests everything that had happened. After meeting with the elders and conferring together, the chief priests offered the soldiers a substantial bribe and told them to say, "His disciples came by night and stole the body while we were asleep." They added, "If this should reach the Governor's ears, we will put matters right with him and see that you do not suffer." So they took the money and did as they were told. This story became widely known, and current in Jewish circles to this day.

The eleven disciples made their way to Galilee, to the mountain where Jesus had told them to meet him. When they saw him, they fell prostrate before him, though some were doubtful. Jesus then came up and spoke to them, He said,...[109] To you who are my friends I say: Do not fear

---

[109] Matthew 27: 62-28:18

those who kill the body and after that have nothing more they can do.[110] If the world hates you, it hated me first, as you know well. If you belong to the world, the world would love its own; but because you do not belong to the world...the world hates you. Remember...: a servant is not greater than his master. As they persecuted me, they will persecute you; they will follow your teaching as little as they followed mine.[111]

It is a fine thing if a man endures the pain of underserved suffering because God is in his thoughts.[112] Even gold passes through the assayer's fire, and more precious than perishable gold is faith which has stood the test. These trials come so that your faith may prove itself worthy of all praise, glory, and honor...[113]

What credit is there in fortitude when you have done wrong and are beaten for it. But when you have behaved well and suffer for it, your fortitude is a fine thing in the sight of God.[114]

My brothers, whenever you have to face trials of many kinds, count yourselves supremely happy, in the knowledge that such testing of your faith breeds fortitude, and if you

---

[110] Luke 12: 4
[111] John 15: 18-21
[112] I Peter 2: 19
[113] I Peter 1: 7
[114] I Peter 2: 20-21

give fortitude full play you will go on to complete a balanced character that will fall short of nothing.[115]

No one under trial or temptation should say, I am being tempted by God; for God is untouched by evil, and does not himself tempt anyone. Temptation arises when a man is enticed and lured away by his own lust; then lust conceives, and gives birth to sin; and sin full-grown breeds death.[116]

Happy the man who remains steadfast under trial, for having passed that test he will receive for his prize the gift of life promised those who love God.[117]

Full authority in heaven and on earth has been committed to me. Go forth therefore and make all nations my disciples;… and teach them to observe all that I have commanded you.[118]

To him who is victorious I will give the right to eat from the tree of life that stands in the Garden of God.[119]…to him who perseveres in doing my will to the end, I will give authority over the nations—that same authority which I received from my Father.[120]

---

[115] James 1: 2-4
[116] James 1: 13-15
[117] James 1: 12
[118] Matthew 28: 18-19
[119] Revelation 2: 7
[120] Revelation 2: 26-27

Chapter 9

He grew up before the Lord like a young plant whose roots are in parched ground; he had no beauty, no majesty to draw our eyes, no grace to make us delight in him; his form, disfigured, lost all the likeness of a man, his beauty changed beyond human semblance, He was despised, he shrank from the sight of men, tormented and humbled by suffering; we despised him, we held him of no account, a thing from which men turn away their eyes. Yet on himself he bore our sufferings, our torments he endured, while we counted him smitten by God, struck down by disease and misery; but he was pierced for our transgressions, tortured for our iniquities; the chastisement he bore is health for us and by his scourging we are healed. We had all strayed like sheep, each of us had gone his own way; but the Lord laid upon him the guilt of us all. He was afflicted, he submitted to be struck down and did not open his mouth; he was led like a sheep to the slaughter, like a ewe that is dumb before his shearers. Without protection, without justice, he was taken away; and who gave a thought to his fate, how he was cut off from the world of living man, stricken to the death for my people's transgression? He was assigned a grave with the wicked, a burial-place among the refuse of mankind, though he had done no violence and spoke no word of treachery, Yet the Lord took thought for his tortured servant and healed him who had made himself a sacrifice for sin; so shall he enjoy long life and see his children's children, and in his hand the Lord's cause shall prosper. After all his pains he shall be bathed in light, after his disgrace he shall be fully vindicated; so shall he, my servant, vindicate many, himself bearing the penalty of their guilt. Therefore I will allot him a portion with the great, and he shall share the spoil with the mighty, because he exposed himself to face death and was reckoned among transgressors, because he bore the sin of many and interceded for their transgressions.[121]

His purpose in dying for all was that men, while still in life, should cease to live for themselves…[122]

He committed no sin, he was convicted of no falsehood; when he was abused, he did not retort with abuse, when he suffered he uttered no threats, but committed his cause to the One who judges justly.[123]

Remembering that Christ endured bodily suffering, you must arm yourselves with a temper of mind like his. When a man has thus endured bodily suffering, he has finished with sin, and for the rest of his days on earth he may live, not for the things that men desire, but for what God wills.

---

[121] Isaiah 53: 2-12
[122] II Corinthians 5: 15
[123] I Peter 2: 22-23

You had time enough in the past to do all the things that men want to do in the pagan world. Then you lived in license and debauchery, drunkenness, revelry, and tippling, and the forbidden worship of idols. Now, when you no longer plunge with them into all this reckless dissipation, they cannot understand it, and they vilify you accordingly; but they shall answer for it to him who stands ready to pass judgement on the living and the dead.[124]

Here is the message we heard from him and pass on to you: that God is light, and in him there is no darkness at all.[125] ...but men preferred darkness to light because their deeds were evil. Bad men all hate the light and avoid it, for fear their practices should be shown up.[126] If we claim to be sharing in his life while we walk in the dark, our words and our lives are a lie; but if we walk in the light as he himself is in the light, then we share together a common life...

If we claim to be sinless, we are self-deceived and strangers to the truth. If we confess our sins, he is just, and may be trusted to forgive our sins and cleanse us from every kind of wrong; but if we say we have committed no sin, we make him out to be a liar, and then his word has no place in

---

[124] I Peter 4: 1-5
[125] I John 1: 5
[126] John 3: 19-20

us. My children, in writing thus to you my purpose is that you should not commit sin.[127]

Here is the test by which we can make sure that we know him: do we keep his commands? The man who says, "I know him," while he disobeys his commands, is a liar and a stranger to the truth; but in the man who is obedient to his word, the divine love has indeed come to its perfection.

Here is the test by which we can make sure that we are in him: whoever claims to be dwelling in him, binds himself to live as Christ himself lived.[128]

---

[127] I John 1: 5-9
[128] I John 2: 3-6

Chapter 10

Thus says the Lord... I am the first and I am the last, and there is no God but me.[129]

The commandment that I lay on you this day is not too difficult for you, it is not too remote. It is not in heaven, that you should say, "Who will go up to heaven for us to fetch it and to tell it to us, so that we can keep it?" Nor is it beyond the sea, that you should say, "Who will cross the sea for us to fetch it and tell it to us, so that we can keep it? It is a thing very near to you, upon your lips and in your heart ready to be kept.[130]

He who loves his neighbor has satisfied every claim of the law. For the commandments, "Thou shalt not commit adultery, thou shalt not kill, thou shalt not steal, thou shalt not covet," and any other commandment there may be, are all summed up in one rule, "Love your neighbor as yourself." Love cannot wrong a neighbor; therefore, the whole law is summed up in love. [131]

---

[129] Isaiah 44: 6
[130] Deuteronomy 30: 11-14
[131] Romans 13: 8-10

Today I offer you the choice of life and good, or death and evil.[132] …If it does not please you to worship the Lord, choose here and now whom you will worship.[133]

---

[132] Deuteronomy 30: 15
[133] Joshua 24: 15